SING OUT LOUD

BOOK I

Discovering Your Voice

Jaime Vendera &
Anne Loader McGee

Vendera
Publishing

VENDERA PUBLISHING

Interior Design by Daniel Middleton | www.scribefreelance.com
Cover Design by Molly Burnside | www.crosssidedesigns.com
Photo detail: Emi Jo Hammond and Kirk Gilbert
Copyright © 2011 by Kevin Hoops | Impressive Studios
Cartoon Illustrations by Jerry Bingham | www.JerryBingham.com
Pencil Drawings by Valerie Bastien
Audio examples recorded by Jaime Vendera

ISBN: 978-1-936307-08-1

Published in the United States of America

Books by Jaime Vendera
*Raise Your Voice Second Edition
*The Ultimate Breathing Workout
*The Ultimate Vocal Workout Diary
*Voice RX
*Vocal RESET
*Online Teaching Secret Revealed
*Unleash Your Creative Mindset

Books by Anne McGee
*Strengthening Your Singing Voice (Elizabeth Sabine)
*The Mystery at Marlatt Manor
*Anni's Attic

Contents

Introduction   7

CHAPTER ONE: Are You Ready to Sing?   9

CHAPTER TWO: YOU Are an AMAZING Instrument!   11

CHAPTER THREE: Your Sound Generator   14

CHAPTER FOUR: Your Fuel Supply   16

CHAPTER FIVE: Using Your Amplifier   24

CHAPTER SIX: It's Time to Catch the Buzz   31

CHAPTER SEVEN: How Many Voices do You Have?   37

CHAPTER EIGHT: Shine with Vibrato   40

CHAPTER NINE: The Sing Out Loud I Workout   42

CHAPTER TEN: Practice Tips   47

ABOUT THE AUTHORS:
   Jaime Vendera   50
   Anne Loader McGee   51

Introduction

Welcome to *Sing Out Loud Book I: Discovering Your Voice,* the first book in the *Young Musician's Series,* written for beginning and professional singers alike. This book is geared towards students from the ages of twelve to eighteen, but anyone of any age will benefit from this program. The *Sing Out Loud* series was created to help establish the basic foundation of vocal technique and help aspiring new and young singers discover their true singing voice. Whether your goal is to run around your house singing at the top of your lungs, stand out in your choir, enter a talent contest, or become the lead singer in a band, the *Sing Out Loud* series will teach you the basics of singing to get you started on the vocal path to success.

Sing Out Loud Book I teaches you the basics of vocal technique and will show you how to begin finding the voice hidden inside of you by vocally experimenting with a wide variety of unusual, but familiar sounds. Once you've discovered your voice and mastered the basic vocal technique for creating and sustaining your sound, you will move onto the next level. In *Sing Out Loud Book II,* you'll begin a rigorous training program to help build those vocal muscles, and in *Sing Out Loud Books III & IV,* you'll get into singing and performing.

It doesn't matter if your current level of singing expertise is 'seasoned vocalist' or that you've never held a note in your life, because the same vocal techniques work for everyone! If you're as excited as we are about learning to sing properly, let's get started on this amazing journey.

Special Note: This book comes with a series of audio files, which were created to guide you through the vocal examples in this book. (**All bold words in parenthesis**) refer to an accompanying audio track, which you'll find at: http://venderapublishing.com/sing-out-loud-book-I/

Now, let's get started!

Chapter 1
Are You Ready to Sing?

Are you ready to rock the stage? Great! But don't get too excited yet. There is much to cover before you become a singing sensation. Throughout the *Sing Out Loud* series you will be required to complete many assignments that are designed to take you to the next step in your singing career. In fact, it's already time for your first assignment.

Assignment #1—Sing Every Day

Singing every single day is one of the keys to becoming an amazing vocalist. But that key won't unlock your singing potential if you don't enjoy singing. Well, there's more to it than just having fun, but without that fun factor, you'll lack discipline, skip practice, and you'll never master your voice. Speaking of practice, you must enjoy the exercises as well. We have to admit exercises can be boring, but if you tackle them like you're singing a song, the exercises will be a blast. With the right attitude you'll discover it's a lot of fun improving your voice.

Everybody is born to sing!

Yes it is true; you were born to sing. The moment you were born and released that first scream, your parents most likely thought you were destined to become the next American Idol. Every baby has the natural instincts for singing because singing is simply the ability to use your breath to sustain speech with lots of emotion. If you've ever heard a baby crying, you know that child has an amazing set of pipes.

Being able to sustain words is what separates the speaking voice from the singing voice. So in essence the two are closely related. Singing allows the listener to focus on the pitch and colors of your voice as you sustain a melody. So you could say that singing is simply sustained speech.

To better understand the basic difference between regular speech and sustained speech let's try an exercise. Repeat this sentence, "Hello, how are you doing?" Next, repeat the phrase while sustaining the vowels. It should sound like, "Heloooooooh, hoooooow aaaaaaaar yuuuuuu dooooeeeeng." **(Sustained Speech)**

Now that you've listened to your first audio track and tried this exercise, you've officially started your vocal training. Having fun yet? Good, because at this point we want to explain how you'll know when it's not fun. It is never fun when it HURTS to sing, which leads us to the golden rule of the *Sing Out Loud* system.

If it hurts to sing, You are doing something wrong.

Always remember the golden rule when imitating the sounds in *Sing Out Loud Book I*. Your voice should never hurt when doing the exercises. In fact, when each sound is done correctly it should feel like you've had a vocal massage.

Pain in the throat or a sore throat afterwards means that you are doing something wrong, which is causing you to strain your voice. If at any time during the assignments your throat begins to hurt, please stop and review the book to make sure that you are following each assignment correctly. Once you are comfortable and feel you have mastered an assignment, you can move on to the next one. Remember, these vocal techniques are used by several of your favorite singers so if you follow the guidelines and exercises in the *Sing Out Loud* series, then you, too, will master these same techniques.

Are you ready to rock? Then let's move on.

Chapter 2
YOU Are an AMAZING Instrument

Your voice is an instrument just like a guitar, piano, flute, or trumpet. It is the best instrument ever made, because it is part of YOU! Like any instrument, you'll never learn to play it well if you don't master the basics. If you are a guitarist, you can recall how you had to learn to tune the strings and strum the basic chords before you could play a song. It's the same with your voice; you've got to learn the basics of singing before you can sing well. The common mistake most new singers make is in thinking they are singing (playing their instrument) correctly because they can vocalize along with their favorite tune.

Just imagine if when you got your first guitar, you pulled it out of the box, figured out all the chords to a song, (although you'd never played a chord in your life) and instantly played along, note for note. You'd probably pat yourself on the back because in your mind it would sound like you played the song perfectly. Since you are under the assumption you are an amazing musician, you decide not to bother practicing at all because you have mastered your instrument. In your mind, practice would seem like a waste of time. Unfortunately, that's not how it works.

Most guitarists put in hours of practice to master their instrument. A practiced guitarist learns how to use unique passing chords, add unusual dynamics, and create moving melodic rhythms, all with precision, feeling and emotion. That's the type of guitar player who will hold an audience spellbound. Singers can learn a lot from a serious guitarist.

Many singers have adopted the "I'm a pro" attitude thinking that they can "play" their instrument right out of the box. Just because you can sing along to your favorite song, doesn't necessarily mean you are playing your instrument correctly. Want proof? Record yourself singing along with a song, and then listen back to critique your performance. While you are listening, pretend it's someone else singing and critique your recording honestly. So, how did it sound? Would *you* listen to you? And even if you did think it sounded amazing, there is always room for improvement.

Whether you like how you sounded or not, it is important that you save your recordings. As you work through *Sing Out Loud Books I-IV*, future assignments will require you to sing the same song several times as you progress through the system so that you can compare older/newer recordings. Comparing versions of the same song will allow you to hear how much you've improved since the very first day you started mastering your vocal technique. On that note, it's time for the next assignment.

Assignment #2—Record a Song

Now it's time to pick, record and critique your song. Don't worry about preparing; just record it so that you can have a recording of what you sound like before you start your training. You can record the song using computer software, a digital recorder, cell phone, video camera or webcam. It doesn't matter how you do it; just get some kind of recording done. In fact, video is the best choice because you can watch your body, face, and neck, which will tell you a lot about your singing technique.

After you record your song, save the file to your computer by creating a new folder entitled, *Sing Out Loud*. You will be recording the same song many times during the *Sing Out Loud* course, so make sure to label and date each version chronologically.

Assignment #3—Critique Your Song

Once you've recorded your song, listen back several times to critique your performance. Make a list (use a program like WordPad) for what you liked and disliked about your performance. There are no wrong answers and it doesn't matter if you end up with more dislikes than likes. Some dislikes may be that you mumbled the words or sang out of key. Some likes may be that you liked your vibrato, or the tone of your voice.

Remember, for a truly honest critique, you should pretend that it isn't you singing the song. Ask yourself, "Would I listen to that singer? If your answer is 'no", then what advice would you offer that singer to help them improve? Add your singing advice to your critique list. Once you've finished your critique, save the document to your new *Sing Out Loud* folder, naming and dating it to match your audio recording. This will create files like the following:

Song Name_ 11_11_2011.mp3 (your audio recording)
Song Name_ 11_11_2011.rtf (your critique document)

Back to the guitar example: once you've mastered the basic chords, you're usually anxious to play your first song. If you're a rock n' roller, you probably plugged your guitar into an amplifier, cranked up the volume, adjusted the treble/bass knobs, and jammed out with enough noise to rattle your neighbors' windows.

A singer's body replaces a guitarist's whole setup. It acts as the instrument, amplifier and treble/bass control. When we know how to work our body/instrument, we can play all the notes, adjust the volume, and tweak the treble and bass controls to create the perfect sound.

The terms 'treble' and 'bass' simply refer to your tone, which is the *color* of your voice. A bass tone has a deep, booming color, whereas a treble tone has a thin, bright color. To a certain degree, the shape and size of your body determines your tone and can affect how you sound. Some people have big, robust tones, while others have thin, flute-like tones.

Once you've mastered the *Sing Out Loud* vocal techniques you'll be able to enhance your tone by adding more rich vibration or "resonance" to your voice. This will allow you to create a variety of tonal colors that you can use to make your singing shine.

Enough talk about guitars, amps and tone; it's time to begin mastering your voice by learning three simple steps. These three steps will turn your instrument into a powerhouse vocal machine:

- *Correct Breathing*
- *Proper Vocal Support*
- *Perfect Vocal Vibration*

All three steps work in conjunction with each other to produce a strong instrument. After you've mastered these three steps, you will be able to protect your voice from strain, increase your vocal range, and enhance the quality of your sound. We'll explain what we mean in the following chapters, but before we do this, let's discuss how sound is created.

Chapter 3
Your Sound Generator

Sound is created down inside your windpipe (trachea) by a tiny little part of your body called the vocal cords. The vocal cords are like guitar strings, which vibrate to create sound. The vocal cords reside inside your larynx, which is also known as your Adam's apple. The vocal cords are attached at the front end of your larynx, but open at the back, forming a **V** shape. When you inhale, the **V** opens up to allow air to pass through. Whenever you speak or sing, the vocal cords come together to vibrate along the edges to create your sound. The sound will also vary in pitch depending on how fast the "strings" (vocal cords) vibrate.

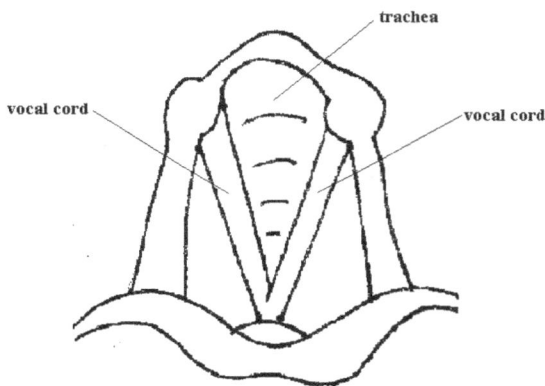

To sum it all up, every note you speak or sing is produced by the vocal cords, which reside down in the throat (the larynx). The vocal cords are tiny, measuring little more than a quarter to a half-inch in length, yet they have the ability to produce amazingly powerful sounds.

Some people think females don't have this Adam's apple the way males do, but if they didn't have one then they wouldn't have a voice. It's just that a girl's Adam's apple doesn't protrude out in the front of the neck the way it does on a boy. To feel your Adam's apple, place the tips of your fingers across the front of your throat, like our friend Kirk Gilbert is doing in the picture on the right. Yawn and then swallow. You'll notice that a little bump moves down when

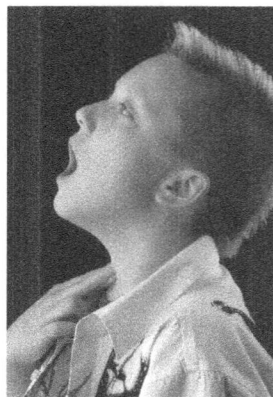

you yawn, and up when you swallow. The position of the Adam's apple can affect the tone of your voice. A low larynx will make you sound like Yogi Bear and a high larynx will make you sound like Bart Simpson. Your goal is to keep the Adam's apple (larynx) in the middle of your throat, which is where it sits when you are breathing normally.

Now that you know how the vocal cords make sound, you may wonder how they can change pitch. To discover the answer, let's try an experiment. Get a rubber band, stretch it between your fingers, and then strum it, like the picture below. You'll first hear a sound, and then see the rubber band vibrating. This is exactly what happens to the vocal cords when air passes through them. Next, stretch the rubber band to different lengths as you continue to strum it. You'll notice that just like your vocal cords, the pitch rises as you stretch the rubber band longer, and lowers when you shorten the length. (**Strumming the Rubber Band**)

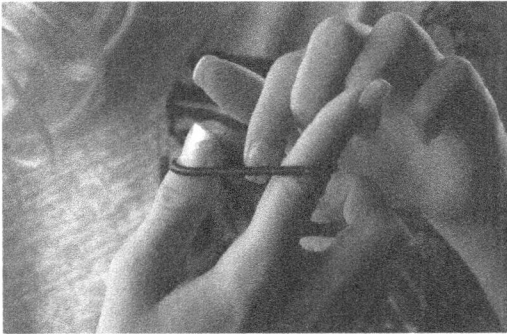

Knowing every detail of how the voice works will not make you a better singer, but having a basic understanding of the vocal cords is important. Even more important is to know how to release the air needed to get the cords vibrating properly. Air is the singer's fuel and in the next chapter you'll learn how to fill up your fuel tank and gauge your fuel release for an effortless sound. Let's move on.

Chapter 4
Your Fuel Supply

If you want to become a great singer, you must know how much fuel (air) to put into your fuel tank (lungs) and how much fuel to release when you sing. Failing to master the fuel process can lead to vocal problems such as strain or vocal loss. Too little fuel will prevent your vocal engine from running well, and too much will literally *blow* up your engine. That's why you MUST learn how to inhale and exhale the right amount of air so that you stay *fuel-efficient*.

In normal everyday breathing we inhale around 3000 gallons of air per day into the lungs. The diaphragm, the dome-shaped muscle that rests at the bottom of the ribs, controls inhalation, and whenever you inhale, your diaphragm contracts and expands downward creating a vacuum within the lungs, which draws in air. When you exhale, the diaphragm begins to relax, which releases the vacuum in the lungs and allows the air to be released through the air tube (trachea), up between the vocal cords, and finally out through the mouth.

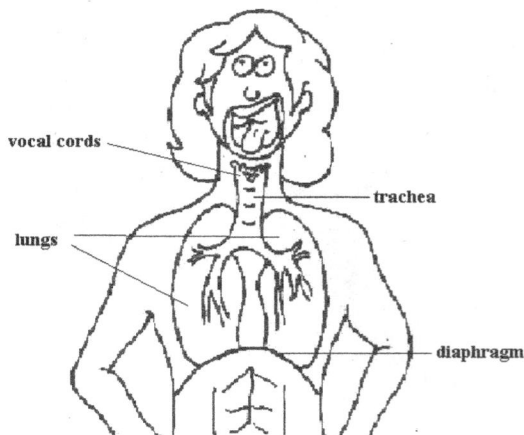

Breathing while singing is a precise art form that singers must master. This breath support takes place when air is released and the diaphragm creates resistance against the opposing abdominal muscles. When you can do this well, you will be able to create the vocal energy needed for a powerful voice. The process may sound complicated but don't worry, it's much easier to do than to explain. So let's jump into the art of breathing and learn how to breathe from the ground up.

You know how to breathe; you've been doing it your whole life, but unfortunately, somewhere along the way most of us have forgotten how to breathe *naturally*. Natural breathing is the secret to amazing vocal power. To rediscover your connection to natural breathing, let's start by inhaling, or filling up your tank.

There's only one correct way to get air into your tank and that's by doing it SILENTLY! You never want to drag air in over the vocal cords or they will become dry, swollen and painful. And you certainly don't want to sound like Darth Vader when you inhale. If you hear yourself noisily sucking in air, then you are doing something wrong.

To inhale correctly, open up your throat by pretending to yawn and dropping your jaw slightly, like our friend Emi Jo Hammond is doing on the left. You'll notice that your air tube has expanded wider in your throat, making it easier to inhale. When you inhale on a slight yawn, imagine that you are drinking in a "quiet" cupful of air. The air will effortlessly slip down the throat like a refreshing drink of water. If you can still hear your breath, you need to continue practicing the quiet breath.

Give it a try. Take a long, slow breath, inhaling in on a slight yawn. At the same time, open your mouth wide and drink in a big cupful of air until you've had your fill. While taking in this deep, full breath, listen closely to make sure you are doing it quietly. Continue practicing this until you're sure you are inhaling properly.

In case you're a bit confused by how wide to open your mouth, the proper mouth position must be as wide as the picture of Emi Jo above, or wider. When you use a slight yawn it raises the soft palate (the dome-like shape in the roof of your mouth) and lets air flow down your throat like a waterslide.

And how do you know how much air to take in for singing? Just enough to get you through the phrase or line you are singing. If you listen closely to your favorite singer, you can probably hear when he or she takes a breath. It's usually at the end of each line of the verse or chorus. Sometimes it's easy to hear the breath and sometimes it's not, depending on how quietly the singer does it. Even some of the pros make noise when they breathe. We bring this point up to let you know that just because a singer is being played on the radio, it doesn't necessarily mean they are singing correctly.

If your favorite singer *is* singing correctly and you cannot hear them taking a breath when you listen to their song, you should still hear a pause in between each line of their verse or chorus. That's where you want to take your breath for that song. As long as you have enough air to get through the vocal line or phrase and still have enough time to take the next breath, you are good to go on fuel. With time and practice you'll learn to adjust your breathing to comfortably match every song you sing. Famed vocal coach Elizabeth Sabine was a master of breathing. Here's a quote about breathing from her book, *Strengthening Your Singing Voice*:

*There are some singers who take breaths at incorrect points in a song, such as in the following example: "I woke the other **night from a (big breath) dream**". It's important to find enough breath in your body to complete the phrase. If you need to sustain the word "dream", take a breath after the word "night". But if you master your vocal technique you can usually sing two full lines because you learn to use very little breath.*

Assignment #4—Filling Up your Tank

Elizabeth is correct. It's about using very little breath. But before you learn how to use minimal breath, you first need to learn how to fill up your tank. Getting that breath under control takes lots of work. So your next assignment is to practice getting that quiet breath down into your fuel tank (your lungs). To do this you must sit down and for the next twenty-five breaths, concentrate on drinking in that quiet breath. Remember, if you inhale on a slight yawn it will lift the palate and the air will slide right down your throat like a drink of water.

Now that you've finished your assignment, you need to know there's more to inhaling than just taking a silent breath. You have to fill your tank from the bottom up. To do this, imagine your body is a balloon and every time you inhale you fill your balloon body up with water. If done correctly, your belly, back and ribs should automatically puff out the same way a balloon does when it is filled.

This might feel slightly weird because most singers don't expand their stomachs out when they inhale; they usually raise their shoulders up and/or puff out their chest. The "puffer chest" syndrome is called chest breathing and limits your fuel supply because it only fills the tank up about one-quarter to one-third. With chest breathing you'll easily run out of breath before the end of each phrase and struggle to make it through the entire song. If you find yourself running out of air in the middle of a song and your face is turning red from trying to hold out all the notes, then you'll need to master the correct techniques of breathing.

To help you understand the concept of using the diaphragm to expand the belly, back, and ribs outward, let's go back to our balloon analogy. When you fill up a balloon with water you'll notice it fills from the bottom up. Think of your lungs filling with air in the same way. Imagine the air going to the bottom first. In fact, imagine you have a giant set of lungs that go all the way down below your belly button. Let your belly, back and ribs expand out as the air pours all the way down to the bottom of these giant lungs. If your ribs and belly expand out without any forced effort on your part, then you are inhaling correctly.

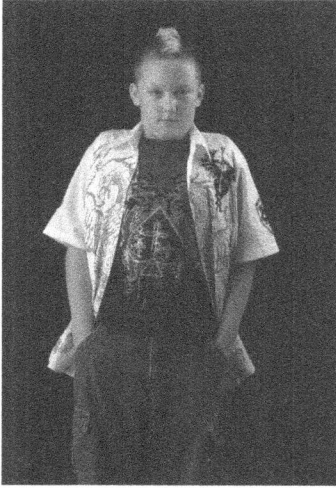

Assignment #5—Inhaling 101

Now it's time for the full correct breathing technique. Stand in front of a mirror so you can watch yourself as you practice this assignment. Take in a deep breath and then immediately exhale until you feel as if you are completely empty of air. Repeat this full in/out breath several times as you watch yourself in the mirror. What moved on your body? If your chest puffed out and/or your shoulders rose up, like Kirk's in the picture to the left, then you are a chest breather, which is the incorrect way to breathe.

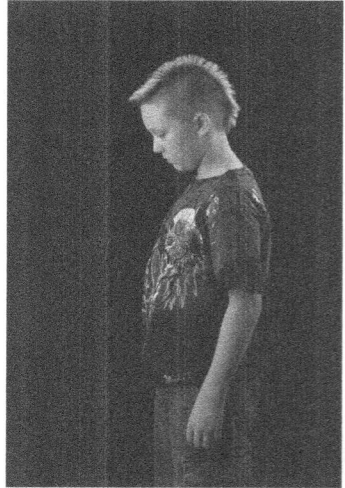

Now, if when you watched yourself in the mirror, your belly, back and ribs expanded out, then you inhaled correctly and are on your way to becoming a more powerful breathing machine. You can see in the picture to the right that Kirk has corrected his breathing pattern, which is now evident because his belly has expanded outwards and his shoulders are relaxed.

Don't worry if you haven't mastered your breath techniques yet because it takes time to correct old breathing habits. Once you've viewed yourself in the mirror several times, and corrected yourself as needed, you can move on to the next assignment where we'll add some exercises to begin building your breathing machine.

Assignment #6—Breathing Exercises

The following exercises will help you master your breathing technique. Practice them once per day, five days a week for the rest of this book.

Exercise #1—Book on Belly

Lie on the floor and place a medium-sized book on your stomach. Take a slow, deep breath and make the book rise up as you inhale.

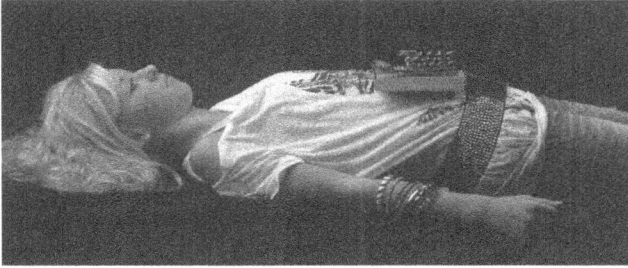

Inhale

Next, exhale and allow the book to drop back down to its starting position as your belly relaxes and lowers.

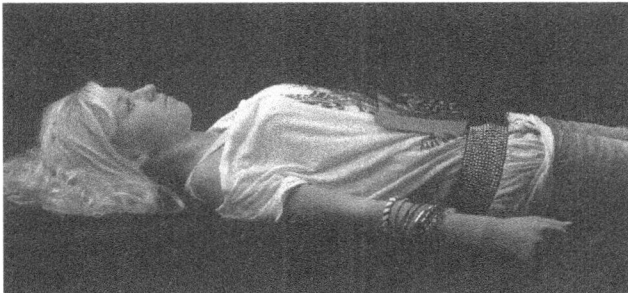

Exhale

Practicing this exercise while lying on the ground prevents the chest from expanding and the shoulders from rising up, which happens if you're a chest breather. Practice this exercise for ten minutes.

Exercise #2—The Hiss

For this exercise, you'll need a timer. While standing up, place your hand against your belly, and then drink in a cupful of air on a yawn. At the same time, focus on filling the lungs from the bottom up, which will expand out your belly, back and ribs.

Once you have filled your tank up with air, push in against your belly (below your navel) by using your fingertips. At the same time tighten your stomach to resist the inward pressure from your fingertips. As you hold this opposing resistance, begin hissing the air out.

As you hiss, you want to tighten your stomach as if you are pushing down like going to the toilet. But you must never make a grunting sound, like being constipated. If you grunt, it will feel like you are locking breath in your throat, which means you are doing it wrong. You should *never* feel it in your throat. This *going to the toilet* or *pushing down* sensation is the key to your breath support, which we'll discuss more in the next chapter. Practice the hiss exercise several times until you can feel the stomach tension without any throat tension. **(Hiss)**

Now once you've got the hang of the exercise, it's time to grab your timer. We're going to see how long you can sustain this hiss. Don't feel bad if you cannot sustain the hiss for very long the first few times you try this exercise. With practice, you will be able to sustain for longer and longer periods of time.

As you reach the end of your breath, you'll notice your stomach muscles begin to burn. That's good because you want to 'feel the burn'. It means you are strengthening your breathing muscles.

Practice the hissing exercise ten times in a row per day. Make it a goal to practice this exercise until you can sustain the hiss for one whole minute. The longer you can sustain the hiss, the easier it will be in the future to sustain notes and sing without running out of breath.

Exercise #3—Blow Up a Balloon

Now it's time for some serious breathing work. Have you ever blown up a balloon and felt tired or dizzy afterwards? That's because you were working three parts of your body at the same time—the stomach, the diaphragm and the lungs, which flooded the body with oxygen and worked the abdominals. So, for this exercise, you'll need to buy some balloons. Don't buy little ones; get some whoppers!

Once you've got your balloon in hand, take in a full breath on a yawn, expanding the belly, back and ribs. Fill up the lungs completely. Next, blow up the balloon as large as you can, then release the air. If the balloon pops, you'll need a larger one. As you blow, make sure to push down like you are going to the toilet. Quickly filling up a balloon helps the brain and body to develop a good breath support pattern, which commits the process to memory. It also strengthens the abdominals and back muscles. Repeat this exercise twenty-five times in a row. Blow up your balloon, release the air, and repeat.

The three breathing exercises in this assignment are just the beginning of building your breathing machine, but they are an important beginning, because they train new breathers to master the art of filling the tank (your lungs) and releasing your vocal fuel (your air). If they seem simple and boring, that doesn't mean you can skip them or that they aren't working. Keep in mind that this is JUST the beginning. *Sing Out Loud Book II* will take you to the next level of breathing. Continue practicing the exercises every day until you move on to *Sing Out Loud Book II*.

Congratulations! Now that you've mastered the art of inhaling and exhaling you've actually learned the first two steps to the *Sing Out Loud* vocal technique. You've already mastered two-thirds of the process. See how effortless it was! Now it's time to begin learning about that all-important third step. This step is so crucial that it will take the next two chapters to teach it to you. So, without further ado, let's move on and learn how to apply your newfound breathing techniques.

Chapter 5
Using Your Amplifier

Although you've already learned some great basics for breath support, there's still more to this fantastic breathing machine than just inhaling and exhaling. It is also the heart of your amplification system. Once your breath support is in place, you must begin feeding vocal energy to the correct places within your body so you can "amplify" your sound.

To better understand amplification, let's look at a guitar amplifier. When starting out, every guitarist wants to crank up their amplifier to eleven—even though it only goes to ten! A smart guitarist soon learns that extreme 'crankage' in volume will damage the speaker. To prevent the speaker from blowing up, the guitarist quickly learns to dial in the right amount of amplification so he can be heard yet not ruin one of his most prized and expensive possessions.

Singers must learn to increase/decrease the volume in much the same way. Without a sufficient supply of air, you'll never be heard, but too much air will blow up your "vocal speaker". By adding just the right amount, you will fill the resonating cavities of your body with sound and resonance (vibration). This in turn will increase your volume without forcing you to shout in order to be heard. And learning to control your volume will prevent you from losing your voice.

What are the resonating cavities, you ask? They are the spaces within your body that vibrate with the sound of your voice, such as your chest and head. But we'll give you more info on this later. Back to the amplifier...

Your amplifier is your body. It serves to control how much or how little volume or energy is released when you sing. Without this "energy supply" the only sound that would come through your vocal cords would be a whiney "buuzzzzzzz" like a gnat. We need to turn that small "buuzzzzzzz" into a large "BUUUUZZZZZ", and the only way to do that is by turning on your internal amplification system.

Many singers think that the amplification system is controlled by breath alone; but it's quite the contrary. Volume isn't created by forcing out more air, or by belting out each note. Volume is created by using your WHOLE body as the amplifier, which allows the singer to increase the volume without increasing the amount of breath being released. This is the secret to real vocal power.

Vocal power comes from using the diaphragm and abdominal muscles—the breathing muscles that feed the sound to all the right places in the body, including the resonating cavities. When you learn how to use these muscles correctly you'll become a powerhouse of sound.

Before moving on though, you need to understand that muscles in the body do one of two things. They contract or they relax. When they contract, they give off energy. So the secret to turning on your amplifier is in knowing how to use your singing muscles to create more energy. And how do you do that, you may ask? Well, you actually learned how in the last chapter. It's step two in the *Sing Out Loud* technique. You tighten your stomach muscles by pushing down like you're going to the toilet. And you continue to hold that downward pressure all the way through your song.

Think of the downward pressure as your power switch. Every time you open your mouth to sing, you need to flip on the power switch in order to create vocal energy. Make sure not to grunt when you do this, because as we said before, grunting stops the flow of vocal energy. It's like folding a hose in two to stop the flow of water. The throat must remain open and free to release the sound. You'll know you are pushing down correctly if you can poke your belly with your hand and the stomach muscles feel as solid as a rock, while the throat feels free of constriction.

Assignment #7—Flipping on the Power Switch

The easiest way to flip on the power switch is by letting out a quick hiss of air. Begin by taking in a quiet breath on a yawn, expanding the belly, back and ribs, and then making quick hissing bursts of air. With each hiss you should push down like you are trying to pass gas. Go ahead, we know you want to laugh. Now that you've had a good giggle, let's try doing ten quick hisses. Don't forget, the stomach muscles should tighten with each hiss as you apply the downward pressure.

To make sure you are flipping on your switch, place your fingertips into your belly as you do this exercise. Hold the fingers firmly in place to give the stomach muscles something to resist against. You will feel your fingers being pushed out with each hiss as you push down and tighten your stomach. As you release air, the fingers will begin to move in as the tank is emptied and the belly returns to its normal position, but the muscles should still remain tight. Perform this exercise ten times in a row. (**Turning on your Amplifier**)

Now that you've flipped the power switch to the ON position, you have to keep it in the ON position. You can do this by keeping the belly, back and ribs expanded, and keeping the abdominal area tight by pushing down. If you relax the stomach area, then the diaphragm will relax too quickly and you'll lose your air supply. Like the stomach area, the back and ribs will eventually return to their normal position as the tank empties. This is normal, but try to keep all three areas expanded as long as you can.

Assignment #8—The Belt Exercise

The exercise in this assignment will help you learn how to maintain expansion in the belly, back and ribs. To begin, tie a belt midway around your ribs. Take a deep breath and make the belt expand by expanding your belly, back and rib cage. Pretend that the ribs are fish gills as you lift them outward. Next, hiss the air out and push down. Focus on the expansion but don't let your shoulders rise up.

This exercise is actually showing you how to turn your diaphragm into a speaker box, which allows the voice to shoot up and out of the mouth without hurting the throat. You'll soon understand the importance of rib expansion and how it affects the sound of your voice. Perform this exercise ten times in a row. Once you feel comfortable with the belt exercise, begin expanding your ribs in the same manner so that whenever you sing, you turn on your speaker box.

Once you've turned on your speaker box, the throat will automatically start to spin vocal vibration and continue to build as it resonates within your body. This vibration amplifies the "loudness" of your voice depending on the amount of energy you can bring up from the abdominal area by pushing downward.

This action will send the vibration sailing out over your vocal cords, and when it spins freely, will automatically be directed up into the roof of your mouth. This is the reason we have you yawn as you inhale. A slight yawn will lift the soft palate up, which in turn creates a home for the spinning vibration. You don't want sound to get trapped down in your throat, and you can prevent this from happening by lifting the palate and focusing the sensation of vocal vibration up there. If you inhale on a yawn, slightly drop the jaw and push down before you sing. The spinning vibration will easily float right up into the palate and never get stuck in the throat, which means that you can eliminate strain.

In case you think all this pushing down and tightening of the stomach is pure brute force, think again. Singing softly takes the same energy and effort as singing loudly. You use the exact same muscles in the exact same way (pushing down), but at a lower volume. In fact, it actually takes a lot more energy to sing softly than to sing loudly because the flow of air is minimized and you must master the ability to keep the air flow very consistent in order to keep the vocal cords vibrating. Speaking of volume, let's move on to the next assignment where you'll learn how to adjust your amplifier.

Assignment #9—Adjusting Amplifier Volume

Since we're discussing volume, let's tackle some new exercises that will teach you how to turn the volume of your power amplification system up or down.

Exercise #1—The Robot

The robot exercise will help you discover how to hold the air back and feel the sensation of vocal vibration in the roof of your mouth. Simply pretend you are a robot, and speak in a very monotone, robotic voice. **(The Robot)**

If you don't know what to say, repeat this whole paragraph with your robot voice. You'll notice it will feel as if there's a metallic, buzzing sensation against the roof of your mouth. This is resonance, which is a result of the spinning vibration of your vocal cords vibrating against the roof of your mouth. And that's where you ALWAYS want to feel it. You'll also notice that it doesn't feel like any air is being released. It feels as if all your air has turned into energy and is buzzing against the roof of your mouth. Don't worry if you can't feel this vibration in the beginning. With each proceeding exercise, you will start to feel it more and more. After you've done the robot exercise, move on to the next one.

Exercise #2—The Baby Cry

Have you ever seen a baby lying in the crib crying when it was either hungry, wanted attention or needed changing? It never went hoarse or lost its voice, did it? That's because babies are born knowing how to use their amplifier correctly. **(Baby Cry)**

As we get older, we sometimes forget how to use our amplifier. To get our memory back, let's take the time to mimic a crying baby. Breathe deeply on a yawn, fill the belly from the bottom up and then push down as hard as you can, as you begin to cry. Cry out like you are angry or want attention. Once you connect your voice to that downward pressure, you will release an enormous amount of energy that will spin up into the palate and let you turn up the volume. This way you can release enormous power from your voice without hurting your throat. You'll also notice with each cry that it will feel as if it is shooting right up and through the soft palate. Once you are all cried out, do Exercise #3.

Exercise #3—The Guinea Pig

Now, let's turn down the volume as low as we can by imitating the small whimper of a guinea pig. In order to create this sound, close your mouth as if you're going to hum and use just enough breath to make the sound squeak out of you. **(Guinea Pig)**

You'll notice that you can create these sounds very softly while adding as much downward pressure as you want, which proves that volume isn't just about tightening the stomach muscles. Now that you have practiced low and loud volume exercises, lets move on to the last exercise of the assignment.

Exercise #4—The Crescendo/Decrescendo

It's time to learn to adjust the volume of your amplifier from low to high and back again. Sustain a "yah" as in the word "father". Start at your lowest volume and then increase the volume as loud as you can without straining. Turning up your amplifier is accomplished by pushing down harder, while feeling more buzz in the roof of your mouth. But that's not all there is to it; you must feel the buzz in your entire body like you were a giant speaker. As you push down and increase the buzz in the roof of your mouth, feel as if the sound is coming out of your legs, your stomach, your chest, your head; your ENTIRE body! Feel the buzz everywhere. You are a giant tuning fork, so use it to your advantage. Once you've increased the sound as loud as you can comfortably go without hurting your voice, turn the volume back down again. As you decrease the sound, feel the buzz also begin to dissipate. **(Crescendo/Decrescendo)**

If you aren't grasping the body amplifier analogy, watch a guitar amplifier up close (while covering your ears, of course). As the amp is turned up while someone is playing, you'll notice that the louder the sound gets, the more the speaker will rattle and shake. When doing this exercise, visualize your body rattling on the loud volumes, just like a guitar amplifier. Remember, when you go loud, do NOT overdo it and hurt your voice. You don't want to blow out your vocal speaker. Go as loud as you comfortably can without hurting your throat. Then decrease the volume back down again as softly as you can without whispering.

The four exercises in this assignment prove that the entire body is used to adjust your volume. Remember, it takes more than pushing down to gain volume; it takes mucho resonance, or entire body buzz. If you rely on a tight stomach alone, you will hurt your voice. The body-buzz and the buzz in the roof of your mouth allow the spinning vibration to build effortlessly until you are vibrating like a giant tuning fork. So catch the buzz and save your voice.

Now that you have a head start on understanding the body buzz, it's time to discuss each of your resonating cavities. Let's move on to the next chapter.

Chapter 6
It's Time to Catch the Buzz

So far we've covered breathing, support, and amplification techniques, so now we believe you are ready for the next step in amplification and tone adjustment, which is adding the *buzz*. The buzz is by far the most important singing SECRET of all because it's the guide that lets you know you're singing correctly. The buzzing sensation is what is often called resonance. We've discussed the buzz (resonance) many times throughout this book already, but now it's time to fine-tune your understanding of it.

So what is resonance? Resonance is that big, full sounding vibration that you hear whenever you sing in the shower. Do you notice how your voice sounds bigger and fuller in the shower? That's because the sound of your voice is bouncing off the smooth reflective surfaces of the shower walls, and this in turn creates a choir of sound bouncing around in the bathroom. Your voice bounces around in the resonating cavities of your body in much the same way.

The key to a good quality sound is building up the resonance within those resonant cavities. You can build your resonance by combining two sources:

- Palate Buzz—continual buzz against the roof of the mouth
  &
- Body Buzz—buzz that moves throughout the body

Let's start with the body buzz, since you've been buzzing the roof of your mouth for several chapters. The body buzz occurs in different parts of your body as you sing and it's what helps make your voice sound fuller. So where does this body buzz occur? When singing a low note, you'll notice that your chest vibrates. This is called low voice buzz or chest resonance. When people sing in the lower part of their range it is often referred to as chest voice because of this buzz. When singing high, you'll feel the majority of body buzz up in your noggin. High voice buzz can make your head rattle or make you feel slightly dizzy. It's often referred to as singing in the head voice.

Regardless of whether you sing high or low, you should still feel your whole body vibrating. But there will always be a spot in the body where the body buzz is strongest. Just as we stated, body buzz will be stronger in your chest on low notes, and stronger in your head on high notes. Don't forget the palate though; whether singing high or low, you should ALWAYS feel the spinning vibration of your voice buzzing against the roof of your mouth. If you learn to combine the body buzz with the palate buzz, you will free the voice of any strain and become an incredibly powerful singer.

Let's jump back to the "palate buzz". We are sure you understand this already, but it's important to review. By feeling the buzz in the roof of the mouth, you'll know for sure that your vocal machine has turned your fuel (air) into power and transformed it into vocal energy. Your voice won't be breathy, won't sound pinched or strained, and you will have a nice tone. So, our goal here is to keep the body and the palate buzzing simultaneously. Remember, palate buzz will always be in the palate, and body buzz will move around depending on how low or high you sing. Catching the buzz will make it effortless to sing and you'll definitely sound better. Now it's time for another assignment.

Assignment #10—Catch the Buzz

To actually create and feel that buzz, first, put your hand on your chest and hum on a low note. You should be able to feel strong vibrations in your chest. Now sing a high note and feel it rattle around in your brain. (**Low and High Buzz**)

To help understand this buzzing sensation, make a fist with your hand, leaving enough room in your clenched fist to push a straw through the center. Next, put your fist up to your lips and begin sustaining an *"ooo"* sound as in the word "you", through the center of your hand. If you are doing it correctly, you will feel vibration inside your hand. This is the same sensation you want to feel on the roof of your mouth and throughout your body when you sing.

Assignment #11—Buzz in the Roof of the Mouth

Now that you've experienced the buzz in your chest, head and hand, it's time to once again practice feeling the buzz against the roof of your mouth. You've most likely already experienced the buzz against the roof of the mouth with the robot and baby cry exercises, but there is always room for improvement. The following exercises will help to find, enhance, and maintain the buzzing sensation.

Exercise #1—Humming Swell

Begin humming with your mouth closed, allowing the hum to swell until it's buzzing against your teeth and the inside of your mouth. Think of Frankenstein's monster saying "mmmmmmmm". You'll notice that your cheeks, nose and entire face, including your ears, buzz and tickle. In fact, it might even make your nose and ears itch. This is a sign that you are doing it right. (**Humming Swell**)

Exercise #2—The Owl

Next, let's hoot like an owl, *"Whoo! Whoo! Whoo!"* When you make this sound, you should feel little bursts of air against the roof of your mouth. These little broken bursts of sound should feel like you're sending Morse code: *"dit, dit, dah, dah, dit, dah"*. Try it again, hooting like an owl on a high, light note. (**The Owl**)

Exercise #3—The Monkey

Using the clenched fist position, go, *"Ooo! Ooo! Ooo!"* like a monkey. You should feel resonance both in your fist and in the roof of your mouth. (**The Monkey**)

The owl and monkey sounds are both created using your falsetto. Falsetto is produced when your voice is high and sounds like a cartoon mouse. Falsetto is also referred to as the false voice because it doesn't sound like your real voice, it sounds more like a cartoon character. **(Falsetto Example)**

Now back to our monkey sound. Can you feel the sound of your voice bouncing off the roof of your mouth? You must feel this sensation before moving on because this sensation is a sign of a correctly produced vocal note. So practice these sounds until you feel that spinning vibration against the roof of the mouth.

Once you've felt the buzz against the roof of your mouth, you should focus on always feeling the buzz whether you are speaking or singing. It's easy to maintain the buzz when you add your downward support. You should feel the buzz whether you sing low or high, use your falsetto, or use your full voice, which is your speaking voice. The *Sing Out Loud* motto is "Catch the Buzz". Catch it in the roof of your mouth and keep it there.

If the buzz is still not there after practicing sounds like the robot, baby cry, owl, and monkey noises, make sure that you are breathing and supporting correctly, as this might be the reason why you've lost the connection to the buzzing sensation. Use a mirror to make sure you are breathing correctly, sticking your fingers in your belly to check for support, and practicing the belt exercise as a guide for proper belly, back and rib expansion. Still not feeling the buzz? Okay, let's try another exercise.

Exercise #4- The Hearty Laugh

Laughing shoots the voice right up into the roof of your mouth. So open up your mouth wide and laugh like crazy. Give a big hearty laugh using your whole body. With each laugh, push down for more emphasis. This kind of laugh will produce lots of vocal energy. **(Hearty Laugh)**

Speaking of vocal energy, you should know that the voice is one big ball of energy waiting to be released. If it's not released in a controlled way, it will go all over the place. This would be the equivalent of giving your kid brother or sister a whopper-sized energy drink to chug down and then turning them loose to wreak havoc in your bedroom. They'd go bouncing off the walls, tearing up everything in sight, and once the drink wore off, they'd hit the floor for a nap and you'd be stuck cleaning up all the mess.

If you let your vocal energy go wild by shouting out when you sing, making every word super breathy, or screaming at the top of your lungs, the notes will fly everywhere. If you are not focusing on your vocal technique, you won't feel the buzz, which is a sure sign you aren't singing correctly. By the time your song is over, your voice will be really, *really* tired and will refuse to do what you want it to do. It would be the equivalent of taking that nap. Your voice will then need to rest to undo any vocal damage. Lack of control may also cause you to go hoarse or lose your voice.

This lack of control over the voice is like unleashing a huge blast of water and not being able to control it. Have you ever had a garden hose with a leaky nozzle? Well, if you did, I'm sure you found out in a hurry that when you turned the tap on full blast, water shot out all over the place, including on you. A proper nozzle always lets you focus the water on a specific point. Your specific vocal point is ALWAYS the palate. By learning to focus the voice into your palate, you won't lose any of the beautiful energy coming out of you.

Let's stop for a moment and review what you've learned so far:

- To fill your tank, you must inhale quietly on a yawn, filling the lungs from the bottom up, and expanding your belly, back and ribs
- To turn on your amplifier, you must push down to tighten your stomach muscles for support
- To increase your resonance, you must *feel* the body buzz like a tuning fork, with the majority of buzz in the chest on low notes, and in the head on high notes. Simultaneously, you must feel the buzz in the roof of your mouth (palate) at all times

Once you can combine all three steps, you will be on your way to mastering your instrument and becoming a singing superstar. However, before moving on to the next chapter, we highly recommend that you go back and revisit all the previous assignments. Practice makes perfect and we want to make sure you've mastered all three steps. Once you've reviewed your assignments you can move on to learn about the different amazing voices you can create.

Chapter 7
How Many Voices Do You Have?

Honestly, you only have one voice, but there are many terms that refer to the different vocal ranges and colors of your voice that are important to know. Have you ever heard someone say, "he's using too much *chest voice*" or "that singer has a great *head voice*" or "I can't seem to eliminate my *vocal break*". These are typical vocal terms, which refer to the different registers or pitches of a singer's voice. In this chapter we'll discuss a few of these terms so you can start building your vocal vocabulary. Many singers get confused about these terms so it's important to have a grasp of the basic terminology. Let's get started.

Chest Voice

The chest voice is the same as chest *resonance*, which we discussed earlier. When speaking or singing in the chest voice, the body buzz will feel the strongest in your chest. To help get this buzz, imagine you've just swallowed a hundred fat bumblebees; the kind that are friendly and won't sting you of course. Feel them buzzing around in your chest like a hive of bees.

Remember, in order to have a great voice, you must be able to feel those fat bees buzzing around in your chest as well as against the palate. To experience the sensation of chest resonance, we'll revisit assignment #10 from the last chapter. Sing a low "aaahhhh" making sure to keep the throat open and focusing on a strong buzz in the chest. Place your hand on your chest and you will feel the buzz. (**Chest Voice "Ah"**)

Another VERY important part of singing in the chest voice is to lift your ribs out. Expanding the ribs makes it easier to reach those lower notes. Although you already know that expanding your ribs is part of the process, it's even more crucial in the lower range if you want to produce bigger low tones. If necessary, practice the belt exercise again.

Head Voice

The head voice is also known as the high voice, as you already know, and notes sung in the head voice tend to sound thinner than low notes. You won't feel much chest buzz on high notes, but you might feel dizzy when you sustain notes in your head voice because the resonance in the head makes the resonating cavity of the skull vibrate. Some people sing all their head voice notes in falsetto because they cannot sing high in their real voice, or full voice. For fun, let's hold out an "aaahhhh" on a high note; move those fat bees right up inside your noggin and let them buzz around like crazy; just don't let them give you a headache. (**Head Voice "Ah"**)

Falsetto

We've mentioned falsetto many times, but let's review this term more fully. Falsetto is your "false" voice and can be created by imitating the voice of a cartoon mouse. It may sound "mousy" and/or breathy, but when perfected, it can give you a cool tool to use at different times when singing. It offers you a choice of a different vocal *color* or sound. Listen to singers like Justin Timberlake and Christina Aguilera. They both use their falsetto on occasion. (**Cartoon Mouse Voice**)

Full Voice

What is the full voice and how does one produce it? Well relax, you already do. It's the sound of your regular voice, or as we mentioned earlier—your speaking voice. You use it every day. It is the basis of your true singing voice. There's nothing wrong with using falsetto to add color to your singing and your goal should be to mix it up between the two voices. (**Falsetto/Full voice example**)

Regardless of which voice you use, falsetto or full voice, chest or head voice, it is still all YOUR voice and all one. With practice, you'll seamlessly blend them all together without any vocal break. It may seem hard at first to think you can have an amazing voice from your lowest note to your highest note without your voice cracking or breaking, but if you practice the exercises and sounds in this book and begin using the vocal workout from

Sing Out Loud Book II, you WILL master your voice!

But how is this possible? How can a singer's voice effortlessly go from the low range to the high? Because you are a musical instrument with mechanical parts that allow you to effortlessly slide from note to note, thereby eliminating any vocal break. What's the vocal break you wonder? Well, be patient, the explanation is coming up next.

The Vocal Break

The vocal break is that point in your voice when you cross over from your low (chest) voice to your high (head) voice. The vocal break is the note at which your voice may wobble and crack making you sound like your grandma. It's the point where you will feel the most vocal strain, or where you will feel as if you cannot go any higher vocally and if you try . . . there comes that grandma voice again. In truth, the break is a gear change—the place where the voice switches from low to high, or vice versa.

To find the break between your low voice and your high voice, begin humming on a low note and slide up as high as you can go. There's a point where you'll hear a flip in your voice. That's the vocal break. **(Hum slide break example)**

You can force this break point to move up higher if you use your breath to shout with lots of volume. But that would cause vocal strain and vocal cord damage. By practicing the exercises in *Sing Out Loud* you won't have to shout and you will eliminate that nasty break. The purpose of this chapter was simply to present you with some very basic fundamentals in terminology concerning your voice. No need to get hung up on it though, it's far better to focus on the work needed to become a better singer. So put the "break" away because you'll learn more about mastering it in *Sing Out Loud Book II.* Now, let's move on to vibrato.

Chapter 8
Shine With Vibrato

Have you ever heard of vibrato? It's the slight up and down change in pitch, which if done correctly, can make the voice sound thicker and warmer. But if your vibrato is too fast or too wide, it can sound like a goat in pain!

A singer who has a great vibrato can make all the difference in the world between sounding mediocre and sounding amazing. Some say vibrato cannot be learned, that it can only occur naturally and you either have it or you don't. We beg to differ. While it is true that vibrato is a sign that a singer is singing without strain, it can STILL be learned.

Assignment #12—Vibrato Exercises

The best way to learn vibrato is to jump right in and do it. So, on that note, let's begin.

Exercise #1—The Hearty Laugh & Belly Bounce

This exercise is simply a hearty laugh like old St. Nicolas does with his jelly belly bouncing all over the place. To begin the exercise, take a deep breath and laugh over and over again. The hearty laugh will let you feel that bouncing ball against the roof of your mouth. Even though you've already done the laugh earlier in this book, this time focus more on *feeling* your whole belly jiggle with each laugh.

Although the hearty laugh isn't the true vibrato we want you to master, this exercise will give you an idea of what the vibrato should feel like. True vibrato is when your pitch goes effortlessly down, and then back up again to where it started.

Now that you've revisited the laugh, sing on an "aaahhhh" with your stomach totally relaxed (no downward pressure) while repetitively pushing in on your belly with your hands. It will make the volume go up and down in a continual wave of sound. Don't tighten your stomach or resist your hands when pushing on the belly. (**Hearty Laugh & Belly Bounce**)

Exercise #2—Pitch Vibrato

Pitch vibrato is your true vibrato and you'll develop it naturally as you learn to use your voice correctly. For this exercise, simply sustain an "aaahhhh" and allow the sound to waver up and down slowly. Practice this every day, increasing the speed as you go. In *Sing Out Loud Book II*, we will start adding full vibrato exercises, but for now you need to gain a basic understanding and become good at it. Play with your vibrato throughout the day like it's a game. (**Pitch Vibrato**)

Believe it or not we're almost at the end of *Sing Out Loud Book I* and you've gained a lot of important information, which will prepare you for the next book. Your goal in the coming month is to practice each sound we've covered in this book before moving on. A month of practice will help you discover the sensations you should feel in your body and prepare you for the next level. We've summed everything up in the next chapter and if you work out your voice once a day using these sounds, it will help you master the basic vocal techniques. Don't cheat. Study this book over and over again chapter-by-chapter until you understand the *Sing Out Loud* vocal technique. Practice along with the audio files and sing every day.

Let's move on to the next chapter where we will cover your daily exercise routine.

Chapter 9
The Sing Out Loud 1 Workout

The following exercises are a variety of sounds that we have already covered in this book and a few new ones to push your envelopes. Mimicking each sound will help you discover your true voice and prepare you for a true vocal workout in *Sing Out Loud Book II*. When you mimic these sounds, make sure you drink in a cup full of air on a yawn, expanding the belly, back and ribs outward. Maintain that expansion, and push down to tighten your stomach for support.

Make sure to practice the sounds while standing up. Standing up helps develop your posture. Having good posture when you sing is extremely important. When standing, imagine there is a string attached to the ceiling, which is hooked to your head, keeping your body tall, erect and straight. Remember, don't lift your shoulders.

Now it's time for your workout. The following is a list of sounds with a brief description on each. Review them by listening to the accompanying mp3 audio files, and then mimicking them. Once you've grown accustomed to the sounds, begin doing the entire list in a row, going over each sound three to five times before moving on to the next. Let's get started by first warming up the voice.

Bubbles

Bubbles—lip bubbles or motorboats, whatever you like to call them—are the perfect warm-up exercise. All you need to do is purse your lips together and blow to make a sound like a horse. For this warm up sound, simply make bubbles on any note you wish, making sure to breathe in, fill the belly up, and push down. If you have trouble making this sound, place your hands on your cheeks to keep them from puffing out. Puffer cheeks always cause problems when you're trying to create bubbles. **(Bubbles)**

Pigeons

Imitate a pigeon cooing to produce this sound. It is NOT tongue trills; it does not involve rolling the tongue. Pigeon sounds occur when the uvula repetitively slaps against the roof of your mouth, like someone hitting a speed bag. The uvula is the little thing that hangs down the back of your throat. Run to a mirror, yawn and look in the back of your throat and you'll see it. Your airflow controls the movement of this uvula. It may take some time to develop and may at first sound like you are spitting up, but in time you will master it. (**Pigeons**)

Hums

The sound of a good resonant hum will fill your face with vibration and quickly warm up the vocal cords. You'll not only feel it in your palate, but you'll also feel it in your cheeks and nose, and sometimes in your ears. Allow them all to buzz and tickle. Simply sustain a, "*mmmmmm*" while feeling the buzz in your cheeks, nose and head. (**Hums**)

Creaky Door

This warm up is the sound you make when you first wake up in the morning. It's called *vocal fry*. Try it on the lowest note in your range on an "aaahhhh" sound, and make sure you feel it in the roof of your mouth. (**Creaky Door**)

Hiss

First things first, let's turn on your amplifier with a few hisses to get the stomach muscles warmed up. Hiss out quickly while pushing down. Repeat the hiss five to ten times. (**Hiss**)

Robot

Pretend that you are a robot. Say, "take me to your leader". Feel the metallic buzz against the roof of your mouth. Spend at least a minute talking in this voice to get the sensation of speaking with less breath. (**Robot**)

This last sound finishes your warm ups. Now that you are warmed up, let's move on to the voice-strengthening sounds.

Owls

The owl sound helps you feel the buzz in the roof of your mouth. We've already covered owl sounds. Do the *"whoo, whoo, whoo"* and feel it in the palate. Keep the sound in falsetto. (**Owls**)

Monkeys

Change the owl sound into a monkey sound by making it staccato like *"ooo, ooo, ooo"*. Don't forget to remove the "H" from the word "whoo". Keep the sound in falsetto. (**Monkeys**)

Hearty Laugh

Let out a round of big hearty laughs and feel your belly shake on each laugh while shooting the sound of your voice into the palate.
(**Hearty Laugh**)

Baby Cry

Cry, cry, cry like a baby, making sure to breathe the belly out. Shoot the sound into your soft palate with each cry as you push down. (**Baby Cry**)

Guinea Pig

The guinea pig sound should be produced as softly as you can. It is similar to the creaky door, but higher in pitch. The guinea pig sound allows the vocal cords to begin learning how to reach those higher notes. (**Guinea Pig**)

Kittens

Move from a guinea pig sound to a light sustained *"meeeoowww"* sound. When you imitate a kitten, you only use the edge of the vocal cords. Keep the sound in falsetto and at a soft volume. (**Kittens**)

Dog bark

Try barking like a dog, first low then high. Feel the bark hit the roof of your mouth. This is an extremely valuable sound for teaching you to connect to the raw power of your voice. (**Dog Bark**)

Barking Tires

This is similar to the barking dog but it is a quick high sound just like the sound car tires make when someone peels out quickly. You must make sure you feel the quick release of sound in the palate. (**Barking Tires**)

Elephants

Let's expand on the humming sound we used earlier for a warm-up to feel the high voice. In a big sound, with your mouth closed, roar on an "*mmmmmm*" like an elephant. You will feel the buzzing sound in your face, nose and cheeks. The area involving the nose and cheeks is called the "mask". Many times you will feel vibration in the mask when the buzz is shooting into the roof of your mouth. Vibration in the mask is a sign that you are singing correctly. (**Elephants**)

Howling Wolf

Now we'll open up the mouth and turn the elephant sound into a howling wolf. This is similar to the baby cry but hang onto the sound and sustain a, "*eeeeooooowwww*" like a crying wolf. This is great for connecting with your high notes. (**Howling Wolf**)

Crescendo/Decrescendo

Time to crank up your volume and then turn it back down again using your entire body. While tightening the stomach, feel the vibration increase as you grow louder (crescendo) and then decrease as you lower the volume (decrescendo). (**Crescendo/Decrescendo**)

Vibrato Wobble

Just for fun, let's play with a little vibrato. Follow the example and move the pitch of your voice up and down repetitively. You can do this sound all day long to begin mastering your vibrato and preparing you for the exercises in *Sing Out Loud Book II*. Now let's finish the set with one final exercise, which will help relax the voice after this amazing workout. (**Vibrato Wobble**)

Slide Whistle

Have you ever played with a slide whistle? Most likely you had a bunch of them floating around at a birthday party. Make an "O" shape with your lips and on a light volume using your falsetto, slide up and down and feel your voice relaxing. (**Slide Whistle**)

That's it! You've finished your first full workout. You should end it by doing at least five more bubbles to relax your voice. After you've finished your daily workout you can sing as well. All of these sounds will begin to release your voice and prepare you for the vocal exercises in *Sing Out Loud Book II*. When you practice, use enthusiasm; make every sound exciting and fun. Get into the character of each sound and make it convincing. In other words, become the animal, become the baby, become the robot, and become the squeaky door. If your mom hears you making monkey noises, she should think there's an animal loose from the zoo. That's how convincing you want it to sound. If your parents complain, tell them that it's part of your required homework. Sound experimentation is one of the best ways to develop your ability to sing.

Your voice should feel great by the time you finish these sounds. You should finish your practice session by vocalizing your favorite songs. Practice is very important so we've included a bonus chapter to help make sure you do your best with each practice session. Flip the page and learn the best tips for an outstanding practice session.

Chapter 10
Practice Tips!

Wow, can you believe how much your voice has grown since you've started the *Sing Out Loud* program? What a difference it makes when you learn a few vocal basics and practice a variety of sounds. But this is only the beginning of your journey; there is much more to come. Although this is a very small book, it has introduced you to the world of professional singing techniques. Think of *Sing Out Loud Book I* as your primer, preparing you for the next book in the series, which brings you one step closer to becoming a great singer.

Remember, you MUST spend at least one month of practice before moving on to *Sing Out Loud Book II*. If you do not put in the time to master your vocal basics, working with each sound, making sure to breathe, support and buzz, you won't be prepared for the next step.

To finish out this book, we've provided the following tips to help you get the most out of your practice:

Tip #1—Practice in a Mirror

The mirror is your very own personal vocal coach. It will point out all of your physical mistakes. When practicing the sounds, use your mirror for making direct eye contact to prevent you from looking up, down, or all around as you make each sound.

Don't make any funny faces. Looking away or making faces is a subconscious attempt to physically control your singing voice. You cannot control your voice; it must happen naturally, effortlessly and internally. We know you don't intentionally mean to take control, but the mind has a funny way of dealing with vocal sounds and using a mirror can help you correct certain mistakes before they become bad vocal habits.

Tip #2—Stay FOCUSED

When practicing sounds, stay focused on your vocal technique. Breathe in on a yawn, expand your belly, back and ribs, push down to tighten the stomach, and feel the buzzing in your body and palate. As you practice, do NOT let your mind drift off to other things such as playing baseball, a math quiz, or

dinner. ALWAYS STAY FOCUSED ON PRACTICE! If you don't stay focused and you rush through each sound, you will never improve. Becoming a better singer takes lots of discipline and dedication.

Tip #3—Drink LOTS of Water

Water is to the voice what oil is to a car engine, so drink plenty of it during the day and while practicing. A singer's voice needs water to stay lubricated. Make sure the water you drink is at room temperature. Cold water makes the voice tighten up, which limits vocal range. For each workout session, you need to drink at least one bottle of water.

Tip #4—Take a Weekly Vacation

Don't practice your exercises every day. Take one day off per week and think of it as a vocal vacation. This gives your voice time to rest and build up vocal strength. But keep singing your song daily. That's important.

Tip #5—Physical Exercise

One of the best ways to improve your voice is through physical exercise. Get involved in sports like basketball, baseball, swimming, or tennis. If playing sports isn't your thing, jump rope, bounce on a trampoline or run on the treadmill. Any physical exercise that gets your heart pumping will benefit your voice. When exercising, make sure you breathe correctly. The way you breathe for singing is the same way you should breathe for life. And focusing on breathing while doing cardio will prepare you for the breathing exercises in *Sing Out Loud Book II*.

The only thing left to say now is, CONGRATULATIONS! That wraps up *Sing Out Loud Book I*. You are now on your way to mastering your voice. After you've spent at least a month on your practice guide and feel comfortable with each vocal sound, you can move on to *Sing Out Loud Book II*. This is where we'll review each aspect of singing in more detail, as well as present you with a new exercise program designed to increase your range and power. See you in four weeks.

About the Author
Jaime Vendera

Jaime Vendera is the author of a variety of books and one of the most sought-after vocal coaches on the planet. Using the methods he created, Jaime turned his two-octave range into six octaves with massive decibels of raw vocal power that enabled him to set a world record shattering glass with his voice. When singers need more vocal range, power and projection, or need to build up vocal stamina to perform every night, they call Jaime Vendera. Jaime states that, "none of this would have been possible without God."

Ben Thomas of Dweezil Zappa says that Jaime is the 'Mr. Miyagi' of vocal coaches, while Mat Devine of Kill Hannah considers him more of a 'Yoda.' James LaBrie of Dream Theater said, "Because of my lessons with Jaime, my voice is feeling and sounding better than it has in twenty years. I am spot-on every night. He is the Vocal Guru." Myles Kennedy of Alter Bridge said, "One time during a tour, I was so sick I could barely make it through the set. It looked as if we were going to have to cancel the next show. Jaime spent some time giving me some tips that helped me regain my voice. By the next night, I was able to perform the show. He is fantastic! *Raise Your Voice Second Edition* is THE book for singers. I recommend his books and his private instruction to ALL singers." Jaime can be contacted at www.jaimevendera.com.

About the Author
Anne Loader McGee

Anne has studied with a number of well-known Hollywood singing teachers. She has performed in musical theatre productions and taken classes in songwriting, music, and film at both the American Film Institute and the University of California and Los Angeles (UCLA).

She also co-wrote *Strengthening Your Singing Voice* with Elizabeth Sabine, a voice-strengthening expert whom many famous singers, actors, and speakers have consulted over the last twenty-five years. (www.elizabethsabine.net)

As an award winning children's writer, Anne has produced plays for young people, developed animation scripts, and had a number of short stories published in magazines, and in the Los Angeles Times. Anne's middle grade novels, *The Mystery at Marlatt Manor* and *Anni's Attic* are available at Amazon and Barnes & Noble. You can find her at www.annemcgee.com.

www.ingramcontent.com/pod-product-compliance
Lightning Source LLC
Chambersburg PA
CBHW070111070426
42448CB00038B/2503